# PROMETHEUS BOUND

# AESCHYLUS

# PROMETHEUS BOUND

Translated into English rhyming verse
with Introduction and Notes

by

GILBERT MURRAY

London
**GEORGE ALLEN & UNWIN LTD**
Museum Street

FIRST PUBLISHED IN 1931
SECOND IMPRESSION 1952
THIRD IMPRESSION 1959
FOURTH IMPRESSION 1973
FIFTH IMPRESSION 1976

ISBN 0 04 882013 X

PRINTED IN GREAT BRITAIN BY
LEWIS REPRINTS LTD.
MEMBER OF BROWN KNIGHT & TRUSCOTT GROUP
LONDON AND TONBRIDGE

# INTRODUCTION

THE *Prometheus* has ranked through the ages as one of the most characteristic works of Aeschylus, alike in its simplicity of construction, its stiffly gorgeous language, and its Titanic majesty of imagination. Yet many modern scholars are inclined to deny it to Aeschylus altogether and treat it as something post-classical, composed perhaps on the foundations of the *Prometheus* which Aeschylus is known to have written. The conclusion is, in my opinion, quite wrong, but the arguments leading to it are instructive. "It is not merely that the language presents peculiarities," they argue, "the whole thing is such a mixture of old and new. It is a play for the study, not the theatre. The stage machinery, with its flying griffins and practicable abysses, is surely beyond the powers of a fifth-century producer. The lyrics have none of the severity of early Attic. The thought, in its blasphemous condemnation of Zeus, must be that of a late sophist, not of the pious early tragedian."

This is not the place to deal fully with this chain of reasoning, but I believe the truth is that the *Prometheus*, produced presumably soon after the eruption of Etna in 479 B.C., is not post-classical but pre-classical. The Attic classical movement imposed a sort of puritan severity on poetry as on sculpture and vase painting, and the *Prometheus*, like the *Suppliant Women*, seems to me to belong to a romantic style not yet Atticized.

The lyric metres of this play are practically those used by Anacreon before Attic tragedy existed, and doubtless by Phrynichus too. (Cf. Aristophanes, *Wasps*, 220, 291 ff.) The ambitious scenery and stage machines are also, I would suggest, pre-classical. Aeschylus had used the same or even bolder devices in the *Europa* and the *Soul-Weighing*. Such things were perhaps characteristic of the style of play which Aristotle calls τερατώδης, or "marvellous," and which he finds in "plays about the Phorkides and Prometheus." But the classical stage, in its stern *Sôphrosynê*, gradually rejected mechanical aids and fantastic stage effects, while it concentrated more and more on language, plot and character, with the plain palace background and the conventional dress. Not till about 430 did Euripides reintroduce the *Mêchanê* for the entrance of divine beings, and then only in the last scene of the play, when the action was really over. Even so he did not escape ridicule.

The actual subject of the play, with its passionate and daring thought—or, as some would say, its sentimental sophistry—presents a different question, but here too I think we have before us something pre-classical. We have the daring of an age that has not yet been frightened. If Euripides had said of Zeus the things that Aeschylus says there would probably have been trouble. By his time people were afraid of the solvent and destructive effects of free speculation; in the time of Aeschylus they were still looking to the powers of the human intellect, to reason and free inquiry, as the great emancipators. But I would go further. Not only is the problem presented by the play quite compatible with Aeschylean authorship; the way in which he has formed it out of the raw material that lay before him is extraordinarily characteristic of Aeschylus. He has indeed, in Aristotle's words, "out of little myths and ridiculous language" created tragedy.

There was in Athens a little local fire-dwarf, the patron of smiths and potters, who had an altar, or rather half an altar, in the Potters' Quarter—Hephaistos had the other half—and was honoured by a torch-race once a year. He was called Prometheus, a name which in Greek means "Forethinker," but has been thought to be a Graecized form of the word which appears in Sanskrit as "*Pramantha*"—"fire-stick." The stories about this clever little daemon tell how he tricked the King of the Gods. Zeus hid away fire, but Prometheus stole it and brought it to earth in a fire-stick or reed: i.e. he invented the method of making fire by rotating a hard stick inside a soft. Zeus was angry, and to punish him invented "a worse fire," namely, the first woman, Pandora, to plague mankind. Then the fire-dwarf invented burnt sacrifice. He divided the body of an ox into two parts, a big parcel containing the fat and bones, and a little parcel containing the flesh wrapped in the hide, and gave Zeus his choice. Zeus naturally, though unwisely, chose the big parcel; and that is why men ever since have given the fat and bones to the gods and kept the good parts for themselves. Eventually

Zeus in anger bound Prometheus in fetters and either impaled him, or—as I think more probable—prisoned him inside a wooden post. (*Theogony*, 522.) There is always fire prisoned inside wood. He was afterwards set free by Heracles.

Out of these trival stories Aeschylus has made one of the great problem tragedies of the world. Prometheus becomes the Forethinker who gave man fire from heaven, the champion who will not bow the knee to all-prevailing wrong, but endures till the end shall come. Some students have conjectured that the *Prometheus* of Aeschylus actually inspired the author of the Book of Job with the subject as well as the curious form of his work. The problem of the two dramatic poems is fundamentally the same: how to reconcile a world that is absolutely indifferent to moral values, except in so far as man himself imposes his will upon it, with the supposed wisdom and benevolence of the Being who inspires and controls it. We need not discuss here the many different attempts that have been made by various religions to solve this problem. Aeschylus adopts one which is generally characteristic of the so-called "Saviour Religions." The Ruler of the world is—with or without reason—an enemy of man, a tyrant to be appeased or an offended master; but there is also a Champion of man, a Saviour who defies or helps to appease the Supreme Being, and, in the end, after infinite suffering, prevails. It is difficult to see how he can prevail. Either the Supreme Being must fall, which is the solution in Shelley's

*Prometheus*, or the two Powers must somehow be reconciled.*

Aeschylus, as we have seen in the *Suppliant Women*, apparently chose this latter solution. The two other plays of the trilogy, *Prometheus Released* and *Prometheus the Torchbearer*,† are no longer extant, but there is enough evidence to show that the end was reconcilia- tion. Prometheus endured for the sake of man and the oppressed Elder Gods all the pains that Zeus could inflict; also, Zeus himself "learnt by suffering" the lesson of forgiveness. He set free his old enemies, the Titans; he spared mankind; he invented the right of the suppliant. These two elements are enough in themselves to make possible a reconciliation, but it seems certain that Aeschylus also brought in a third element. From the very beginning Zeus was not quite what he seemed. He was inscrutable; he had far- reaching wisdom, which his enemies and victims had not understood. The best illustration is his treatment of Io, which in this play seems like the caprice of a lustful tyrant, but is eventually revealed—if we may use the *Suppliant Women* to explain the *Prometheus*—as not only guiltless of lust but as a deep-laid plan for leading Io to a state of blessedness otherwise unattainable, and

---

* As I write there comes news of a rising of Africans in the Belgian Congo, who believe that the Devil is coming as a saviour to deliver them from the White Man's government, which of course represents the White Man's God.—*The Times*, June 27, 1931.

† There was also a Satyr-play called *Prometheus the Fire-kindler*, which seems to have dealt with the first discovery of fire, and the discomfiture of a Satyr who tried to kiss the beautiful thing.

even bringing about the release of Prometheus himself. On these lines the mystery does not really disappear. Zeus remains inscrutable. We may ask, as at the end of the *Oresteia*, why, if Zeus is ready to pardon the doer of his will after infinite suffering, he was not ready to pardon him at the beginning. To that Aeschylus attempted no answer; or, if he did, it is lost.

Presumably there is no answer. Job does not give it, nor Shelley, nor Milton in his effort to "justify the ways of God to man," nor any of the theologians. After all, it was not the business of Aeschylus to solve a philosophic problem. What the play does achieve, and a marvellous achievement it is, is to make one feel, not the solution which perhaps does not exist, but the world-agony, the courage, the heroism of love that do exist, and the beauty, in a way better than happiness, that results therefrom. In a sense it is all true; Zeus is true. There is a material world-order, utterly alien to man's ideals, and almost omnipotent over him and them. Prometheus is true. There is a power of the spirit which dares to love and be just in the midst of a world to which such words are meaningless, and thus defies the omnipotent. The Oceanides are true. There is, throughout the human part of creation, and even beyond the human part, an ever-living *compassio*, or σνμπαθεία, a "fellow-suffering" of those not directly affected with those who suffer. These ideas, while the germs of them are present in the Babylonian "Faithful Son," and more elaborate forms of them have become familiar to us in certain doctrines of

Christianity, seem, as far as European literature is concerned, to have found their first expression in the *Prometheus*.

"The whole creation groaneth and travaileth," says St. Paul. I suppose the vast majority of mankind, as long as they are fairly comfortable themselves, do not realize at all the meaning or the truth of these words. To those who do, the *Prometheus* seems to be "telling their own dream."

But meantime, whatever ideas Aeschylus the thinker might wish to suggest, Aeschylus the playwright had to knit together the story of his play. He started with one of the stories in Hesiod, the theft of fire and the punishment; but how was he to arm Prometheus against the All-ruler, how was he to have him eventually released and restored? He meets the first question by using Hesiod's great myth of the Sky-Kings or Year-Kings, and carrying it a step further. Every Year-King is overthrown and supplanted by his son. First came Ouranos (Sky) wedded to Gaia (Earth), who bore to him a son, Kronos, mightier than his father. Then Kronos reigned, wedded to Rhea, who bore to him a son, Zeus, mightier still, who drove out Kronos, and now reigns over the world. Must Zeus fall too? Zeus himself has no suspicion, but Prometheus knows a secret oracle which reveals that the sea-goddess, Thetis, is destined to bear a son greater than his father, and, as it happens, Zeus intends to make Thetis his bride. This knowledge gives Prometheus his power. When reconciled with Zeus he reveals it, and Thetis is thereupon given in marriage to the blameless hero Peleus. Her son of course was Achilles, so that her destiny was fulfilled.

In the current myth, it would seem, Prometheus was eventually set free and forgiven. There was a wreath of plaited willow worn at the torch-race, which was supposed to be a memorial of the bondage which Prometheus had once worn. The stories of deliverance, however, are, as usual in such myths, rather confused. Prometheus is himself a Saviour. In one version he is released by Heracles, the great Saviour, by the will of his Father, Zeus. In another, hinted at in ll. 1027 ff., his Saviour must die for him; Chiron, the divine Centaur, wounded beyond cure by a poisoned arrow, agrees to go to death in his place. Aeschylus adopted the first.

One other addition which Aeschylus had made to the story has often seemed to scholars puzzling and irrelevant. This is the introduction of Io, the Hornèd Moon-maiden, haunted and gadfly-driven, pursued by the hate of Hera. To one who asks the meaning of Io one may perhaps answer in the words of Euripides,

> Nay, know ye not, this burden hath alway lain
> On the devious being of woman? Yea, burdens twain,
> The burden of wild will and the burden of pain.

Io illustrates both. But I will not repeat what I have written in the Introduction to the *Suppliant Women*.

G. M.

# PROMETHEUS BOUND

## DRAMATIS PERSONAE

PROMÊTHEUS, *a Titan, son of Ouranos and Gaia* or *Themis, giver of fire to man.*

HEPHAISTOS, *the God of fire, Latin* Vulcanus.

KRATOS and BIA (MIGHT and FORCE), *Daemons attendant upon Zeus, the King of the Gods, Latin* Jupiter.

OCEAN or ÔKEANOS, *God of the Ocean River which surrounds the world, Father of all streams and rivers.*

ÎO (the Argive name for the Moon), *daughter of the River Inachus, a horned Maiden, beloved by Zeus, and driven wandering across the world.*

HERMÊS, *the winged Herald of the Gods, Latin* Mercurius.

CHORUS *of the Daughters of* OCEAN, *with their* LEADER.

The date of the play is not recorded, but it must have been written soon after the great eruption of Mount Etna in 479 B.C. (Ll. 360 ff.)

# PROMETHEUS BOUND

*The scene represents a desolate landscape. At the back
    towers a great Rock against which stands the
    gigantic figure of* PROMETHEUS. *He is guarded by
    the two Daemons* KRATOS *and* BIA (MIGHT *and*
    FORCE), *who also carry the tools of* HEPHAISTOS, *the
    hammer, chains, fetters and spike of adamant.*
    HEPHAISTOS *stands a little way off.*

### KRATOS.

Here at the furthest verge of earth we stand,
The Scythian pale, a lone and ghastly land.
Hephaistos! Now bethink thee of the charge
Our Father on thee laid: against the marge
Of this sky-piercing precipice to bind,
In gyves of adamant and bondage blind,
This wrecker of the law. 'Twas he who stole
Fire, thine own glory, fire, that is the soul
Of every art, and flung to man away.
For which sin to all heaven he needs must pay
Atonement, till he learn our Master's plan
To accept, and cease this love for mortal man.

### HEPHAISTOS.

O Force and Might, to you the word of Jove
Is all in all; against it naught may move.
But my heart sickens, in this craggy high
And tempest-riven gulf, to crucify

A god, my kinsman.—Yet I needs must find
The heart to do it. Woe to him whose mind
Shrinks from its task, beneath the eternal eyes!
   O child of Themis, meek as she was wise,
Thou dreamer all too daring, though my heart
Is loath as thine I shall perform my part,
Aye, and in bonds of brass indissoluble
Nail thee against this life-deserted hill,
Where never face of man, nor voice, nor name
Shall reach thee. Scorchèd in the midday flame,
Thy scaling flesh shall blacken; thou shalt cry
For spangle-sleevèd Night to veil that eye
Of fire, shalt cry again for Dawn to fold
Back from thy limbs Night's agonies of cold.
Alway the present pain shall be the one
Most hated; and Redeemer hast thou none.
Lo, the reward of all thy love for man!
Thou, child of heaven, hast heeded not the ban
Of heaven, but given a power beyond the right
To them that perish. Therefore, day and night,
This joyless crag alway shall cradle thee
Erect, not closing eye nor bending knee.
And many a groan and cry shalt utter there,
All fruitless: Jove's heart listeth not to prayer.
But conquerors all are hard in the early days.


KRATOS.

Enough! Why these vain murmurs and delays?
Why dost not hate him, this most perilous foe
Of heaven, who flung thy gift to them below?

HEPHAISTOS.
My kinsman, my old comrade . .    tis too hard!

KRATOS.
I know it; but His will to disregard,
Hast heart for that? Wouldst thou not fear it worse?

HEPHAISTOS.
Alas, thou know'st not pity, nor remorse!

KRATOS.
It aids him nothing, to be wept upon.
Why vex thyself with pains that profit none?

HEPHAISTOS.
O craftsmanship, once loved, now hated sore!

KRATOS.
Why hate it? Naught of this thou grievest for
Was caused or aided by that craft of thine.

HEPHAISTOS.
Would God it were another's, and not mine!

KRATOS.
All ways of life are hard, except to be
King of the Gods: since none but Zeus is free

### HEPHAISTOS.
This day I have learnt it, and gainsay thee not.

### KRATOS.
Uprouse thee then, and get the bondage wrought
About him, lest Jove mark thy failing will.

### HEPHAISTOS.
There are the fetters ready.—Gaze thy fill.

[HEPHAISTOS *takes his hammer: they proceed to the work of chaining* PROMETHEUS *to the cliff.*

### KRATOS.
Good!—Clip his arms thy hardest. Now a shock
Of the great smiter! Nail them to the rock.

### HEPHAISTOS.
The work goes ever on. It turns not back.

### KRATOS.
Strike harder. Tighter there; leave nothing slack.
He can find ways out of the deadliest noose.

### HEPHAISTOS.
This arm is fixed: a knot that none can loose.

### KRATOS.
Now pin the other. Let the trickster know
How, matched with Zeus, his quickest wits are slow.

HEPHAISTOS.

I fear no blame save his who hangeth here.


KRATOS.

Now for the spike of adamant, to spear
His breast through; that will hold unshakeably!


HEPHAISTOS.

O brother, can I bear thine agony?


KRATOS.

Shrinking again, and weeping for God's foes?
Thou'lt need thy tears for nearer pains than those!


HEPHAISTOS.

Thou seest this sight that tortureth mine eyes?


KRATOS.

I see a caitiff punished caitiff-wise.
Come; cast about his limbs the swathing bands.


HEPHAISTOS.

I must.—Be not so free with thy commands.


KRATOS.

By heaven, I will, though; aye, and shout, and hound
Thee further!—Climb down. Ring his ankles round.

HEPHAISTOS.

That task gives little labour. 'Tis complete.

KRATOS.

Now hard! The spikèd gyves to pierce his feet!
A reckoner stern awaits; forgettest thou?

HEPHAISTOS.

Ah me, thy tongue is savage as thy brow.

KRATOS.

Weep if thou wilt; but leave to me my mood
Of stubbornness, and my heart's solitude.

HEPHAISTOS.

Let us be gone. He is bound from head to heel.

KRATOS.

Hang there in all thy pride! There learn to steal
The glory that is God's, and cast away
His treasures to these creatures of a day!
Shall man bring help to thee in this distress?
    And the gods called thee, in their foolishness,
Prometheus—the Forethinker? 'Tis that thought
Thou lackest most, now that we have thee caught
By our good craft—a forethought that unbinds!

    [*Exeunt* HEPHAISTOS *and the two Attendant*
        *Daemons.* PROMETHEUS *left alone at last*
        *raises his head.*

PROMETHEUS.

Thou holy Sky, ye swift and wingèd Winds,
And River Founts, and laughter of the seas
Innumerable: Thou, Mother of all these,
Earth, and thou Sun that seest all things, see
What things, being god, the Gods have wrought on me!

In what long tortures, on and on
Through myriad years I agonize:
Such bonds of shame He doth devize
Against me who but now hath won
The throne of blessèdness! Woe's me!
For grief that is and that shall be
I groan; Oh, when and in what guise
Cometh an end of misery?

And yet what say I? Clearly I foreknow
Each pang that cometh: no unlooked-for blow
Can touch me ever, and he who knows for sure
His fate doth best to chafe not, but endure,
One thing being certain, that no victory
Is his who wars 'gainst That which Needs must be
Ah me, I know not how to speak my thought,
Nor leave unspoke: 'tis for that gift I brought
To man that in this torment I am bound.
Hid in a rush's heart I sought, I found,
The fount of fire, to man a shining seed
Of every art and a great help in need.
Behold the sin for which I suffer, high
Enchained, with piercèd heart, beneath the sky!

25

Ha!

What music, what fragrance invisible comes to enfold
    me—
    From god is it wafted, or man, or some being
        between——
To the rock at the world's end? Oh why, except to
        behold me
    In torment, broken? What else can these things
        mean?
    Regard me then in chains, the suffering god,
        The foe of Him who Reigns, foe fore-designed
Of all by whom the floor of Zeus is trod:
        So greatly have I loved mankind.

Ah me!
A rustling in the void I hear,
    As of great birds, and the air sings
    With a soft beat of rippling wings.
All that approacheth makes me fear!

*Enter through the air on winged chariots the*
    CHORUS, *the Daughters of* OCEAN.

CHORUS.
    Nay, bethink thee not of ill:
        It is Love upon the air,
    With a racing of quick pinions, bears us on.
        It was hard to bend the will
        Of old Ocean to our prayer,
But the wingèd winds were waiting, and I panted to
        be gone!

For the beating of the iron, clang on clang,
   Through our deep caverns echoed from afar;
And a great pity shook me, and I sprang
   Unshodden to our tempest-wingèd car.


PROMETHEUS.

O brood of Têthys—great is she
   And many-childed—seed of him
   Whose sleepless river laps the rim
Of the wide world, come gaze on me,
Daughters of Ocean; look on this
   My bondage, how I guard amain
The utmost crag of the abyss,
   A watch-tower of eternal pain.


CHORUS.

O thou Sufferer, I see;
   Though a mist across my eyes
Upriseth, full of tears, full of dread,
   As I mark the form of thee
   To the rocks and bitter skies
In this horror of the piercings of adamant, outspread.


For strange hands are now upon the helm
   Of Olympus; with new doings manifold
And lawless Zeus fortifies his realm,
   And hath cast down the Mighty Ones of old.

PROMETHEUS.

Would that in chains beneath the world,
  Beneath Hades, where dwell the dead,
  To Tartarus the unplummeted,
He had in rage this body hurled,
That neither man might gaze on me
  Nor god, as now when, pang by pang,
  A blown leaf in the wind I hang,
And they that hate me laugh to see.

CHORUS.

Who of all gods hath heart so vain
  To laugh at these things? Is there one
Who doth not suffer with the pain
  Thou sufferest, save Zeus alone,
Who grindeth still, intent on hate,
  The brood of Ouranos o'erthrown,
  And will not spare them till he sate
  His rage, or by some craft unknown
Another seize the unconquerable throne?

PROMETHEUS.

That Lord of Bliss shall need me yet,—
  I swear it—in my chains and woe,
  To warn him of the doom I know
Shall break his sceptre and o'erset
His glories. And no wizardry
  Of honeyed words shall then assuage
  My purpose, no tempestuous rage
Subdue it, till he set me free

From this foul bondage, and atone
In tears the evil he hath done.


CHORUS.

Oh, thou art valiant! None shall teach
    By torment that proud heart to quail.
But all too daring is thy speech.
    My spirit trembles, like a veil
Pierced by the wind. I fear for thee
    What cometh: shalt thou e'er have won
A further shore to this wild sea?
    His ways are fathomless, and none
Shall turn by words the heart of Kronos' son.
[*By this time the* CHORUS *are all at rest in the air.*


PROMETHEUS.

I know that Zeus is hard, I know
    He sees no justice but his will:
    Yet that hard heart, I swear, shall still
Be softened, on the day this blow
Strikes it. Oh, he will smooth again
    His stormy mood, and sue to me
    For compact, yea, for amity,
His fear as galling as my chain!


LEADER.

Reveal thy story now, and tell us clear
For what trangression proved he holds thee here
Prisoned, in such dire torment and disdain.
Speak—unless all such speech to thee is pain.

29

## PROMETHEUS.

Oh, pain indeed my story is to tell,
Yet silence pain, and all ways miserable.
When first the immortals learned the taste of
    wrath,
And strife rose, and between them wound its path,
Many would cast out Kronos from his throne,
That Zeus forsooth might reign, but many an one
Swore that no Zeus should e'er be lord of heaven.
Wise was I, but no force to me was given
To move the brood Titanic, born of Earth
And Sky. All crooked plans they turned to mirth
In their great hearts, and thought full easily
By strength to master all. But much to me
And ofttimes had my mystic mother told—
Themis and Gaia, titles manifold
Of one eternal form—what end must fall:
That in this warfare not by strength at all,
Only by thought, the conquerors should prevail.
I spoke, I showed my brethren all the tale,
But they nor heard my words nor looked at me.
Best then I deemed it, if such things must be,
That I with Zeus, led by my mother's light,
Should stand, will linked with will, in armèd fight;
And by my counsels now the deep and cold
Abyss of darkness covereth Kronos old,
With all his peoples. Such the gift I brought
To Zeus; and this the answer he hath wrought!
In every tyrant's heart there springs in the end
This poison, that he cannot trust a friend.

But for your question, on what charge he so
Hath tortured me, give ear and ye shall know.
When first he mounted on his father's throne
Straightway he called the gods, and gave each one
His place and honours. So he wrought his plan
Of empire. But of man, unhappy man,
He had no care: he counselled the whole race
To uproot, and plant a strange brood in its place.
And none took stand against that evil mind
Save me. I rose. I would not see mankind
By him stamped out and cast to nothingness.
For that he hath laid on me this bitter stress,
This pain which maketh weep those that pass by.
Mercy I had for man; and therefore I
Must meet no mercy, but hang crucified
In witness of God's cruelty and pride.

LEADER.

Oh, wrought of iron, Oh, built of bitter stone,
Prometheus, were the heart that did not groan
For this. Would it had ne'er been mine to see
Such wrong; but, having seen, pain conquers me.

PROMETHEUS.

A piteous sight I am, to all who love.

LEADER.

Was this all? Naught beyond it or above?

31

PROMETHEUS.
From thoughts of coming death I saved mankind.

LEADER.
What medicine for that sickness couldst thou find?

PROMETHEUS.
Blind hopes I planted in their hearts to dwell.

LEADER.
A blessed thing for lives so miserable!

PROMETHEUS.
And further . . . I gave Fire to them that die.

LEADER.
And hath man Fire, that bright all-piercing eye?

PROMETHEUS.
Whence he shall learn all arts, all greatnesses.

LEADER.
Ah me! And is it for such crimes as these   .   ?

PROMETHEUS.
He wrongs me and relents not? 'Tis even so.

LEADER.
And is no end set to thy waste of woe?

#### PROMETHEUS.

None; save the will of him who tortureth me.


#### LEADER.

The will of Zeus—how then? What hope for thee?
Canst see not now, thou hast the law transgressed—
Though any word that blames thee were unblest
For me to utter and for thee mere pain?
Leave that aside, and let all seek amain
Some way to loose thee from this bondage dire.


#### PROMETHEUS.

'Tis well for them whose feet touch not the mire
To chide and counsel the afflicted. Lo,
All that hath come I knew from long ago.
With firm resolve and knowledge I transgressed,
Nor now deny it. Ages of unrest
Must needs be mine, bearing to man his bliss;
Though, sure, I dreamed not such revenge as this,
On this unneighboured hill, amid these high
And desolate crags, would drain my life-blood dry.
  But, prithee, mourn not for my present grief;
Set foot on earth, and let me find relief
In telling of the days to come, that so
From end to end ye may my story know.
Grant me, I pray you, this! So shall ye shed
Comfort on one now sore uncomforted;
For Sorrow, without favour, without care,
Roaming the world, now lighteth here, now there

### CHORUS.

A willing ear hath heard thy cry,
Prometheus. Now with nimble feet
I leave my wingèd chariot-seat
   And the holy sky,
Wherethrough the great birds float and fly,
And on this waste of rock descend;
   Most fain would I
Hear all thy labours to the end.

[*The* CHORUS *descend to earth: at the same time*
   OCEAN *appears thro' the air, mounted on a*
   *flying Griffin.*

### OCEAN.

O'er void unending leagues of road,
Prometheus, to thy need I fly,
Guiding by thought, not curb nor goad,
This wide-wing'd courser of the sky.
On me thy sorrows needs must light,
Being thy kin; and more, I vow,
None is there honoured in my sight
   More high than thou.
The deed shall prove me. Vainly to pretend
Is not in Ocean's nature. Do but show
The way to serve thee, and thou soon shalt know
   Thou hast no trustier friend.

### PROMETHEUS.

Ha!
What means it? Com'st thou also to achieve
Sight of my griefs? How hast thou dared to leave

The flood whose name thou bearest, and the lone
Self-builded caverns of o'er-arching stone,
To seek this iron-embosomed land? Wouldst fain
See how I stand, and sorrow in my pain?
Feast then thine eyes! Thou seest before thee one
Who was Jove's friend, who helped him to the throne
Of heaven, and with these pains he racketh me!

### OCEAN.

I see, Prometheus; and would tender thee,
For all thy subtle wisdom, counsel true.
Oh, know thyself, and clothe thy mind with new
Thoughts. A new god is now the Lord of lords.
And if such jaggèd and keen-whetted words
Thou hurl about thee, though the throne of Jove
Is far, he yet may mark thee from above;
Then would these pains that crowd on thee to-day,
Beside his direr vengeance, seem like play.
Be it not so! Away, O sufferer, cast
Thine angry mood, and seek some road at last
To free thee from these bonds. My words, I know,
Will seem as children's lore, learnt long ago;
To list to them is but part-punishment,
Prometheus, of a tongue too turbulent!
Thou art not humble yet; nor by the pain
He sends thee, softened. Nay, thy heart is fain
For more affliction still! Friend, wouldst thou learn
My rede, thou wilt not stretch thy foot to spurn
Against the goad. Stern-hearted is the king
Who rules us, and abides no questioning.

35

And now I will go plead with him, and strain
All powers I have, to loose thee from this chain.
Only do thou possess thy soul, nor fret
Thy speech to wilder storm.—Hast learned not yet,
In all thy passing wisdom, that there be
Curbs for the mouth that speaketh vanity?

### PROMETHEUS.

I charge thee, be content; thou that hast shared
The plans I counselled and the deeds I dared,
But not my punishment. Therefore, let be
My fortunes; think no more of them nor me.
Thou move that pitiless heart? I do but fear
Now lest he make thee rue thy coming here.

### OCEAN.

Thou takest thought for others in their need
Far better than thyself. 'Tis by the deed,
Not words, I judge thee. Therefore hold me not
Back from this venture when my heart is hot.
Sure am I, sure, Zeus to my prayer will grant
This grace, and loose thy nails of adamant.

### PROMETHEUS.

I thank thee, friend, and will for ever bless
That heart which never fails in faithfulness
And love. But venture not. 'Twere all a vain
Venture for me, thy prayer, and wasted pain,
If pain thou needs must have. Nay, hold thy peace,
And wait in quiet. Would it bring surcease

Of woe to me, if far and wide I taught
Others to share my torment? I trow not.
   Part of my sorrow is the pain of him,
Who, standing at the world's far western rim,
On his great shoulders bears the pillar stone
Of earth and sky, hard weight for one alone,
Atlas, my brother. Yea, another too,
That earth-born shape Cilicia's caverns knew,
I have seen and pitied: Typhon, wild with hate,
The hundred heads in fury subjugate,
Who dared to rise 'gainst all the hosts of God,
His snake fangs hissing and a-foam with blood,
His dark eyes blazing with a fire most like
The lightning in its wrath, as though to strike
God's very throne. Ah, from that throne there came
One sleepless shaft, one thunder-blast of flame,
And silent struck the vauntings of his pride.
The fire had pierced him to the heart, and dried
His life-blood; and away his strength did pass.
And now, a helpless and wide-groping mass,
He lieth fall'n, beside the salt sea strait;
The mountain roots of Etna spread their weight
To enclose him, while far, far, upon the heights
Above, Hephaistos on his anvil smites
The rough red iron; and thence shall break one day
Rivers of fire with ravening jaws, to prey
On the fair fields of fruited Sicily.
So fierce shall Typhon hurl, in days to be,
His wrath and hail fire-scattering, though o'ertrod
And blasted by the levin-bolt of God.

Think, therefore! Thou art not untried in life,
Nor needest me for master. From this strife
Hold thyself safe, by whatso plan of ease
Thou knowest. I will drain unto the lees,
Alone, my cup of fortune, till the pride
Of Him who reigns in wrath be satisfied.

OCEAN.

Yet knowst thou not, when a King's wrath is stirred,
There is no medicine like a healing word?

PROMETHEUS.

If at a chosen hour one seeks to assuage
His anger, not crush down the swelling rage.

OCEAN.

To strive my best for thy sake, and be bold—
What hurt dost see therein? May I be told?

PROMETHEUS.

Vain kindliness, and waste of foolish breath.

OCEAN.

Those frailties I can bear. It profiteth
The wise, foolish to seem and wise to be!

PROMETHEUS.

Thy deed of folly Zeus will charge to me.

38

OCEAN.

Ah!
That bids me turn and leave thee to thy fate?


PROMETHEUS.

Beware!
My love may earn for thee another's hate.


OCEAN.

His who now holdeth the eternal crown?


PROMETHEUS.

Even so. Beware if once thou see him frown!


OCEAN.

Alas, my lesson in thy pains I find.


PROMETHEUS.

Leave me. Begone. Hold fast thy present mind.


OCEAN.

Already, as thou urgest me, I go.
My dragon steed, wide-wingèd, beateth slow
The level paths of sky; glad seeketh he
His home far off and rest beyond the sea.

                                    [Exit OCEAN

CHORUS.

We sigh, O Prometheus, for thy doom of desolation;
  There are tears in the rivers and the falling of the
    rain,
There are soft eyes unseen that uplift thee an oblation,
  In this world of undelight that the laws of Zeus ordain;
For his sceptre it is proud and unbent by supplication
  To the remnant of the old gods' reign.


But every land is loud with a travail of compassion:
  The peoples of the sunset, they go grieving by the
    sea,
For a beauty long ago, for a greatness of old fashion,
  Thine and thy brethren's, in the days when ye were
    free.
In the hordes of holy Asia there is wakened a strange
    passion
  And the lips of them that perish pine for thee.


Yea, the Amazons, the dwellers beyond Phasis,
  Who love not, who battle without fear;
And the riders that wander in fierce places
  At the world's rim, the Scythians of the Mere;
And hard men, of Araby the flower,
  Where the high crags of Caucasus advance,
They groan in their mountain-builded tower,
  Amid great wrath and flashing of the lance


The breakers of the sea clash and roar
Together, and the gulfs thereof are sore

With longing; there is murmur of hearts aching
　In Hades and the Cavern of the Deep,
And the torrents of the hills, white-breaking,
　For pity of thy pain weep and weep.


PROMETHEUS.

Think not from pride, nor yet from bitterness,
I am silent; 'tis old memories that oppress
My spirit, when I see this contumely
And insult cast on me. Who else but I
Did on each one of these new gods bestow
His throne and office? But of that ye know;
I say no more. Hear now the sorry tale
Of mortal man. A thing of no avail
He was, until a living mind I wrought
Within him, and new mastery of thought.
I cast no blame on man; I do but crave
To show what love was in the gifts I gave.
I tell you, sight they had but saw in vain;
Hearing, but heard not; as shapes wax and wane
In dreams, aimless for ever and confused,
They moved; no binding of the clay they used,
No craft of wood, to build in the bright sun
Their dwellings; but like feeble ants wind-blown,
Hid them in crannied caves, far from the day;
No seasons did they know, no signs to say
When winter cold should come, nor flowery spring,
Nor summer with his fruit, but everything
They did was without knowledge, till their eyes
Were oped by me to see the stars that rise,

41

And them that sink to heaven's obscurer parts.
Then Number, Number, queen of all the arts,
I showed them, and the craft which stroke to stroke
Added, till words came and the letters spoke;
The all-remembering wonder, the unworn
And edgèd tool, whence every Muse is born.
Beasts of the forest and the field I broke
To harness, made them servants to the yoke
And carriers who might lift from man the pain
Of extreme toil; I hanselled to the rein
The gentle steed, and in the chariot tied
For rich men who would glory in their pride.
I made, none else, for mariners the free
And flaxen-wingèd chariots of the sea.
Alas, all these new wisdoms I could find
For mortals, but no wisdom to unbind
These mine own fetters—nay, nor hope of it.


LEADER.

Great are thy wrongs: but wherefore should thy wit
So fall despairing? A poor leech is he
Who, falling sick, doth seek no remedy.


PROMETHEUS.

'Tis strange, and will seem stranger when the whole
Tale of my crafts and findings I unroll,
In man's first days. Did any sickness then
Seize them, no medicine was there among men,
Not herb nor draught nor unguent; helpless they,
For lack of healing drugs, would waste away

Even unto death, till I the blending taught
Of gentle balms, whereby a fence is wrought
'Gainst all disease. Aye, more than that, 'twas I
Sorted the divers paths of prophecy.
I was the first to judge of dreams, what kind
Fulfilment bear; I read the inward mind
Of the unintended word and the stray sign
Met by the road. I did the flight divine
Of great and ravening birds, I first did mark
Which held the shining future, which the dark;
I showed their ways, I showed of diverse wings
The feuds and friendships and cohabitings.
I in the deep heart of the victim slain
Revealed what hue, what surface, maketh plain
God's pleasure; a dread shapeliness withal
I made man see in liver and in gall,
Howe'er they changed. I read the burning sign
Of thigh-bone savour-wrapped and tapering chine.
Thus man to knowledge came of things to be,
Deep hid before. Yea, I put eyes to see
Into the face of fire, and gave to him
A fount of vision that before was dim.
So runs that story. . . . And beneath the ground
I saw what hidden helpers could be found
For man's life—bronze and silver, iron and gold.
Who thought of them before me? Who had told
Their names? I wot, none other. Ye have heard
A tale that can be summed in one brief word:
All that of art man has, Prometheus gave.

LEADER.

Ah, think not alway of the deeds that save
Mankind, forgetting thine own misery!
In spite of all, I hope thy bonds shall be
Unloosed, and thou once more like Zeus in power.

PROMETHEUS.

Thou hopest?—Nay, for that the fatal hour
Is not yet ripe. A myriad throes of pain
And wrath shall rack me ere I escape again
This bondage. Art and skill things wondrous are,
But That which Needs must Be is stronger far.

LEADER.

Who guides the helm of That which Needs must Be?

PROMETHEUS.

The Erînys unforgetting, the Fates three.

LEADER.

Then Zeus himself, matched against these, is weak?

PROMETHEUS.

The doom that is ordained he cannot break.

LEADER.

What doom can his be, save to reign alway?

PROMETHEUS.

Ask me no more. Naught further must I say

44

LEADER.

'Tis some dread mystery thou veilest there.

PROMETHEUS.

Enough! 'Tis not the hour for thee to share
That word. Let it lie deep in darkness. So
Only I rise above this shame and woe.

CHORUS.

Oh, never towards Him who ruleth all
    May my thought be shaken from its peace!
At the worship of his altars, at the call
    Of his feasters, may I falter not nor cease;
        By the banks of old repose
        Where our Father's river flows,
May my lips offend not ever, and the law my spirit
        knows
    In piety be firm and increase.

It were happiness to live thus for ever,
    Untroubled, and in hope of things to be,
Making joy by the music of the River;
    But I tremble when mine eyes turn to thee,
        And I know the long chain
        Of thy torments, pain on pain.
Thou hast feared not, thou hast trusted to the thought
        of thine own brain,
    And loved Man so dearly! What is he?

45

Alas, the vain service unrepaid,
O Friend! Whither lookest thou for aid?
   Shall they comfort thee, who perish in a day?
Didst thou see not that Man was ever thus:
Little-doing, and his strength hazardous
   And dreamlike? In such weakness, every way,
His blind tribes are chainèd, and his thought
   Shall escape not the prison, nor outstray
The frame the great Carpenter hath wrought.

I knew it when my eyes oped to see
The evil that is fallen upon thee;
   Then through me, like a wingèd music, glanced
Fear, thrilling; and behold, another song
I remembered, how before thee in a throng
   By the bed and the water-spring we danced,
When home, in the morning of thy pride,
   Thou didst lead through the singing, joy-entranced,
Hesionê, our sister and thy bride.


*Enter along the plain* Io, *a distraught Maiden,
horned like the Moon.*


Io.

What land? What people? Who is he
   Whom thus in bridle-curb of stone
   I see storm-beaten?   . . What hast done
So dire that here they torture thee?
   Answer; and say to what strange zone
I have wandered in my misery.

Ah, Ah!
   Again some gadfly blade
Stabs me. Ah, ghost of earthborn Argos, back!
Hold him, O Mother Earth! I am afraid.
   There with a thousand eyes
He comes . . . on, on. Crafty he is and black,
   And though he is dead, long dead, he never lies
Quiet in the grave. He still will rise, will rise,
Up from the dead, a bloodhound, hunting me
Along the sands, beside the starving sea.

I cannot sleep. The wax-enwoven reed
Pipes on. Oh, whither do these wild ways lead,
   So far, so far? What sin,
O Thou Eternal, didst thou find in me,
   What wickedness within,
To bind on me this yoke of agony
   And madness; and my head
   Pierced with this stabbing dread?
Oh, kill me! Burn me with thy fire; or heap
Earth o'er my lips or fling me to the deep
   To feed the monsters there!
Have mercy, Master, on thy servant's prayer!
   I am so heavy-laden
With weariness, and know not where to fly
   From this long misery.
Oh, hear me; it is I, thy hornèd Maiden!

PROMETHEUS.

Methinks I hear the gadfly-driven child
Of Inachus, who made Jove's bosom wild

With love, and goeth her long pilgrimage
Unwilling, hunted still by Hera's rage.


Io.

Thou speak'st my father's name!
O awful Sufferer, and who art thou,
To accost this wretch aright, to know the flame
God-sent that hath so changed and marred me now,
Stabbing with stings of madness? Starved am I,
    And wronged, and wildly fly
To reach thee, broken by her plots, her hate.
Who, of all them they call unfortunate,
Hath grief like mine? O prophet, tell me plain
    What sufferings still remain;
Knowst thou of help or medicine for mine ill?
Oh, answer! Break thy silence; and fulfil
A virgin's prayer, whose pilgrimage is pain.


PROMETHEUS.

All that from me thou seekest thou shalt hear,
And not in riddles, but as friend speaks clear
To friend, and fully openeth his desire.
I am Prometheus, he who gave man fire.


Io.

Thou star of blessing to mankind! Alas,
What brings thee, most unhappy, to this pass?


PROMETHEUS.

Nay, I have told but now that tale of woe.

48

Io.

So be it.  Yet one thing I fain would know.

PROMETHEUS.

Ask as thou wilt; I will deny thee naught.

Io.

Say who on this wild crag thy bondage wrought.

PROMETHEUS.

Hephaistos lent the hand, and Zeus the will.

Io.

What sin deserved a doom so terrible?

PROMETHEUS.

Enough! That which thou knowest tells the whole.

Io.

Speak, then, of mine own pilgrimage; what goal
Is set thereto? What years must come and go?

PROMETHEUS.

Ah, not to know were happier than to know.

Io.

Nay, hide not that which some day I must see.

PROMETHEUS.

It is not that I grudge to show it thee.

#### Io.

Why art thou shrinking, then, to make all clear?

#### PROMETHEUS.

'Tis but the racking of thy heart I fear.

#### Io.

Ah, build me not more shelter than I ask!

#### PROMETHEUS.

If so thou wilt, so be it!—Hear thy task.

#### LEADER.

Prithee, not yet. Let my wish too prevail,
Till first from her own lips the ruinous tale
Of this sad maid be told, and then from thee
She learn the sum of travails yet to be.

#### PROMETHEUS.

These Ocean daughters to thy father's wave
Are sisters, Io, and the boon they crave
'Tis of thy grace to grant. And surely here
'Twere well to weep away the long-pent tear,
And speak the unspoken tale of wrong. There be
In this waste land who dare to weep with thee.

#### Io.

I know not to deny you; ye shall hear
All that ye ask of me. And yet a fear

50

Even now comes o'er me, speaking of the storm
God-sent, and this distortion of my form
And understanding, on what wings they sped.
For ever hovering o'er my maiden bed
Came visions of the night, and whispered me
Soft words; "O Maid of strange felicity,
Why reject love so long, when thou mayst win
So great a lover? Zeus doth burn within
With longing, and with thee, with thee, doth pine
To uplift the Cyprian's burden. Daughter mine,
Spurn not the kiss of Zeus, but go thy way
To Lerna's meadows deep, where herded stray
The flocks and kine of Inachus thy sire.
So shall Jove's eye have ease from its desire."

By such dreams, eve by eve, being possessed,
At length I sought my father, and confessed
Those fears that wandered in the night. And he
To Pytho and Dodona diligently
Sent herald after herald, so to learn
What offering or what deed of his might turn
God's mind. And each brought back some oracle
Of shifting lips, unclear and hard to spell,
Until at last there came one voice, not dim
Of speech but very clear, commanding him
To thrust me forth from home and fatherland
To wander, masterless, to the last strand
Of the world; and if he would not, there should fall
From Zeus the fire-eyed levin, to cast all
His race to death. As loath as I he was,
But, bowed beneath the word of Loxias,

He drove me from his house and barred the door.
The curb of Zeus it was that held him, sore
Against his will, to do deeds horrible.
Then straightway on my shape distortion fell,
And on my mind; and hornèd, as you see,
Stabbed by the gadfly's poisonous agony,
A maddened beast, to the sweet stream I fled
Of Kenchreae and Lerna's fountain head,
Craving for rest. And there across my path,
That earthborn herdsman, Argos, red in wrath,
Stood watching, with his thousand sleepless eyes.
Him an undreamed of, lightning-swift, surprise
Bereft of life; but still the gadfly's blade
Stabs, and o'er nation after nation, flayed
By that unearthly scourge, I work my path.

   Thou hast heard my story. If some further wrath
Yet waits for me, reveal it; let no ruth
For mine affliction make thee hide the truth
With fables; for I know no human thing
So fraught with poison as false comforting.


CHORUS.

Ah, God protect me! Never did I dream
   To hear so strange a tale: a thing I dare
   Not think nor look upon, yet she must bear:
Wrong, cruelty and horror! It doth seem
To pierce my spirit like a sword, ice-cold.
   Do such things lie in wait
For the innocent? O Doom unguessed, untold,
   I tremble as I gaze on Io's fate.

### PROMETHEUS.

Too soon thou weepest, like a child in fear;
The rest of Io's fate is still to hear.

### LEADER.

Speak, then: show all. The sad heart hath relief
To know for sure the worst of coming grief.

### PROMETHEUS.

The boon ye asked before light labour brought
To me; 'twas from this damsel that ye sought
To hear the conflict strange that hath oppressed
Her life before. Mark now, and hear the rest
Of the Great Goddess' wrath against this maid.

   O flower of Inachus, be not afraid
To write these words of warning in thy soul;
So shalt thou guide thee to thy journey's goal.
From here, first turn thee toward the rising day;
O'er the world's unploughed acres make thy way,
And reach the roving Scyths, whose dwellings are
Of woven reeds, each on his wheelèd car,
And bows far-slaying in their hands. To these
Approach not. List to where the stormy seas
Are breaking, and there cross that evil land.
A clank of iron then on thy left hand
Shall sound; 'tis there the Chalyb tribesmen dwell,
Smiths, fierce to strangers and implacable;
Be wary of them. Next thou shalt bend thy path
Beside a lordly river, named of wrath,

Which pass not—'tis not easy to be passed—
Until to Caucasus himself, the last
And loftiest of mountains, thou art come,
From whose white brows the river bursts in foam,
A torrent spring. Climb there across the bars
Of the great ridges, neighbour to the stars,
And, once across, turn to the southward land.
Thus shalt thou reach the Amazons, a band
Which hateth men; whose squadrons yet shall ride
In Themiskŷra by Thermôdon's tide,
Where Salmydessus' jaw the Euxine grips,
The sailor's bane, a stepmother of ships.
These with all love will guide thee, only these,
To where a gateway of the narrowing seas
The Cimbrian isthmus holds; from thence depart
Onward and traverse with unflinching heart
The strait Maeotic mere. A wondering praise
Of that great deed shall live in after-days
Among mankind, and. in thy memory
Ford-of-the-Hornèd-One that strait shall be.
Thereafter shall thy foot be set no more
In Europe; boundless Asia spreads before
Thy vision. . . . Is He cruel in like wise
Where'er He moves, this Tyrant of the Skies?
He lusted for this mortal maid, and lo,
He hath heaped on her this pilgrimage of woe!
O Maid, a bitter wooer hast thou met
And cruel; for the tale thou hast heard as yet
Is scarce the preface to what still shall be.

[Io *sobs aloud.*

54

Again a voice, a sob, breaks forth from thee:
How when thou hearest thy full tale of pain?


LEADER.

Is this not all? Doth something still remain?


PROMETHEUS.

A whole wide ocean of consuming woe.


Io.

Why should I seek to live? Oh, let me go
Up on yon piercing precipice, to cast
My body to the winds, and so at last
Be rid of evil! Better die the death
Now, than live on with pain in every breath


PROMETHEUS.

How hardly wouldst thou bear such fate as I,
To whom it is not possible to die?
Death to all ills brings respite; but the grief
That I endure shall know of no relief
Nor lightening, until Zeus from heaven be cast


Io.

Can this thing be, that Zeus shall fall at last?


PROMETHEUS.

'Twere joy to thee, methinks, to see that hour?

Io.

How else? I live in pain while He hath power.

PROMETHEUS.

Rejoice then, for these things deep-rooted stand.

Io.

What foe shall wrest the sceptre from his hand?

PROMETHEUS.

His own vain lusts and false imaginings.

Io.

Speak on! Unless to speak some peril brings.

PROMETHEUS.

He woos a bride whose kiss shall be his bane.

Io.

Goddess, or woman? . . . If thou canst, be plain!

PROMETHEUS.

Ask not. That name must not be breathed nor known.

Io.

The wife he weds shall hurl him from his throne?

PROMETHEUS.

Her first-born greater than his sire shall be.

56

Io.

And none can turn from Zeus that destiny?

PROMETHEUS.

I can; but only when these bonds are loose.

Io.

Who could unbind thee, save by will of Zeus?

PROMETHEUS.

One born of thine own blood he needs must be.

Io.

How sayst thou? Child of mine shall set thee free?

PROMETHEUS.

Ten ages pass, then comes the saviour third.

Io.

Alas, I can no longer read thy word!

PROMETHEUS.

Ask not; nor ask what toils before thee lie

Io.

Thou wouldst not grant my boon, and then deny?

PROMETHEUS.

Two oracles I know, and one will tell.

#### Io.

Which be they? Let me choose mine oracle.


#### PROMETHEUS.

So be it; choose. Shall I unveil to thee
Thy wanderings, or the hand that sets me free?


#### LEADER.

One grace to me, and one to Io grant,
And so reject not either supplicant;
First what ways she must tread; then who shall save
Thyself from bondage. That I sorely crave.


#### PROMETHEUS.

I will not steel me to refuse the task
Your love so craves, but speak of all ye ask.
First, Io, of the driven ways and blind
That wait thee—in the tablets of thy mind
Grave thou my words—I tell. Strive boldly on,
Face the sun-trodden fiery ways of dawn,
And cross the deep sea's tumult, till thou win
Kisthênê and the gorgon plain, wherein
The Phorkides, eternal virgins, lie,
Three, swan-like, sharers of a single eye,
A single tooth, whom never ray of light
Findeth by day nor stealing moon by night.
Hard by them their three wingèd sisters wait,
Gorgons, with serpent hair and eyes of hate,
Whom none of mortal kind may see and live.
For thy first road these warning words I give.

58

Thereafter comes another perilous sight:
Beware Jove's death-hounds of the voiceless bite,
The Gryphons, and the Arimaspian breed
Of one-eyed warriors, urgers of the steed,
Watchers who haunt about the golden hoard
Of river-flowing sand by Pluto's ford.
Approach not them. Then to a distant land
Thou comest, coal-black folk on either hand,
Who dwell beside the fountain of the sun,
Where springs the Ethiop River. Pass thou on
Guarding the bank, until thou reach the Falls
Where Nile in flood from Byblus' mountain walls
Outpours his healthful and adorèd flow.
Take him to guide thee to that region, low,
Three-sided, 'twixt the river and the sea,
Where, 'tis ordainèd, by thy sons and thee
The far-off City shall at last be reared.

If there be aught in this that thou hast heard
Too dim, or hard of reading, brood it o'er
And ask. Of time I have enough and more.


LEADER.

If aught remains unspoken or forgot
Of Io's wandering woes, refuse it not;
Else, if thou hast told her all, before thee set
My prayer: 'twas one not easy to forget.


PROMETHEUS.

The last term of her roaming she hath heard:
Howbeit, lest she still may doubt my word,

The earlier travail I will tell, wherethrough
She has passed ere now. So she shall know me
   true.
Not through the whole long story will I wend
My way, but haste me to the journey's end;
Rememberest thou the deep Molossian plain
And skyey-ridged Dodona, where the fane
Of Zeus Thesprotian lies, the throne of state,
And, passing strange, the oaks articulate
With murmuring speech; the oaks that greeted thee
Loud before all mankind, as Bride to Be
Of Zeus? Methinks that stirreth in thy mind.
Then fell thy goad upon thee, and in blind
Anguish pursued thee down the level shore
Of Rhea's boundless gulf, from whence once more
Storm-driven backward thou didst range in flight.
That gulf in after-ages shall be hight
Ionian, that thy wandering to the west
May live.—How say'st thou? Is there in this breast
An eye which sees beyond things visible?
Enough: to you and Io both I tell
The rest, completing tales half-told before.
A tower there is on Egypt's utmost shore
Just at Nile's mouth, amid the pilèd sand:
There Zeus shall calm thy madness by his hand,
Casting out fear, whose touch is all in all.
Therefrom shall spring a child, whom men shall
   call,
In memory of the magic of that Hand,
Dark Epaphos. The fruits of all the land

Which Nile doth water shall be his to hold.
Five generations thence, a fifty-fold
And virgin pilgrimage shall turn again
Most loath to Argos, from the lust of men,
Their kindred, flying. They in passion high,
As hard behind the doves the falcons fly,
Shall follow, grasping that which is not got
By grasping. God shall see, and give them not
The flesh they crave. Nay, Greece for them doth
    keep
A war of armèd women, and a sleep
At midnight doomed by hearts that watch and
    dare.
Each virgin bride shall bring her ravisher
Death, and each whetted dagger claim its own.
Such be mine enemies' wooing! One alone
Of all those damsels her own heart shall charm
To hate not him who clasps her in his arm.
Her purpose she shall break, and deem it less
Vile to be craven called than murderess.
She shall be mother of a royal race
O'er Argos reigning; but 'twere long to trace
The whole strange tale. Suffice it, from that seed
Shall spring a heart most bold, a bow at need
Unerring, famed afar. Io, 'tis he
Who from these bonds at last shall set me free.
So stands the word of knowledge which of old
Titanian Themis to her son foretold;
But how and where, methinks, were a long tale
To tell, and in thy need of none avail.

## Io.

Eleleu!
> Again the spasm, the maddening thrill!
>> Again, like fire, the poisoned dart
>> Stabs, and beneath my breast the heart
> Struggles. Ah God, I cannot still
> The wandering of my eyes! My feet
>> Bear me I know not whither, flung
>> Leaf-like before the wind. My tongue
> Obeys not; my words vainly beat
> Against this flood that beareth me
Out, blind and hated, to an unknown sea.

*[Exit* Io.

### Chorus.

Wise, wise was he to whom the thought first came,
Whose tongue first owned the Law, that Love should aim
> Not at the stars but his own lowly kind:
Not amid delicate damsels rich with gold,
Not in the pride of them with lineage old,
> The toil-worn hand shall dream his bliss to find.

And women there have been, O Fates above,
Who in the bed of Zeus lay, lapt in love,
> Who reached their arms to wooers from high heaven!
I would not be as these were, when I see
Before me Io's cold virginity
> O'er hard and homeless paths by Hera driven.

Let love meet equal love, and fear shall die!
Bend not on me, O ye enthroned on high,

The unassuagèd hunger of your eyes!
All striving then were vain, all hope despair;
I know not how I should be changed, nor where
    Escape the all-piercing thought of Zeus the Wise.


PROMETHEUS.

I swear that yet, for all his stubborn pride,
Zeus shall bow low his head. There is a bride
He woos and wins; and winning, shall be hurled
From that high throne and sceptre of the world
To darkness. Then the curse shall be complete
Which, falling broken from the aeonian seat
Our father Kronos spake. To avert that hour
Is mine alone. No other god hath power
To know what comes and how. . . . Oh, let him there
Sit crowned and fearless, strong behind the blare
Of crashing skies, and ever in his hand
Turning the death-shaft of his levin wand.
Shall these avail him on that day when he
Must fall, dishonoured, irrecoverably
To the great deep? So dire a thing of death
'Gainst him and his even now he gendereth,
A wrestler unaffrontable in fight
And marvellous; who shall make to him a light
More fiery than the lightning, a more loud
Crash than the crashes of Jove's thundercloud;
And that earth-shaking torment of the main,
Poseidon's trident, he shall break in twain.
Then Zeus shall learn, beneath that mastering wave
O'erborne, the difference between lord and slave!

63

LEADER.

Thine own desire 'gainst Zeus so prompteth thee.

PROMETHEUS.

What I desire I speak, and what shall be.

LEADER.

Thou dream'st one cometh who shall master Zeus?

PROMETHEUS.

With yoke like this yoke, but more hard to loose.

LEADER.

Dost fear not, hurling forth such rebel breath?

PROMETHEUS.

How should I fear, for whom there is no death?

LEADER.

Some pain he may devise more torturing.

PROMETHEUS.

I fear not. I know all the years can bring,

LEADER.

Ah, wise are they who kneel in fear of Fate!

64

### PROMETHEUS.

Kneel, worship, fawn on him who now is great!
To me he is less than nothing. Let him do
His will, and lord it this brief season through!
Not long shall he be King in heaven. . . . But stay;
What minion yonder hither bends his way?
The all-obedient servitor of Zeus,
Hermes! Methinks he beareth some great news.

*Enter, flying through the air,* HERMES. *He alights
on a crag high up.*

### HERMES.

Thou over-wise, thou bitterer than gall,
Flouter of Gods, that mortal mán withal
May live, thou thief of fire, give me thine ear!
The Sire commands thee name and make full clear
This bridal which thou vauntest, and whereby
His throne shall fall. Say each thing severally,
And riddle not, nor let this toil of mine
Be vain. Zeus weakens not to pride like thine.

### PROMETHEUS.

Aye, haughty-lipped thy speech, and thy heart brave
With boasting, as befits the Olympians' slave.
I read you well; young gods and new in power,
And dreaming thronèd in a griefless tower
To reign for ever more! Have I not known
From that same height two monarchs overthrown,

E                65

And yet a third shall know, in shame most dire,
Most sudden? Thinkest thou I dread the ire
Of these young gods of thine, or cower before
Their thrones? I take no thought of them. Therefore
Begone the way thou camest! Thou shalt wrest
From me no word of what thou questionest.

HERMES.

So say'st thou? The same stubborn wind again
That bore thee to this harborage of pain!

PROMETHEUS.

My prison chains against thy servitude
I would not change; be that well understood.

HERMES.

Wouldst liefer serve this rock, a chainèd thrall,
Than live true Herald to the Lord of all?

PROMETHEUS.

Here I can meet my mockers, scorn for scorn.

HERMES.

Meseems, thou gloriest in thy fate forlorn.

PROMETHEUS.

Glory! Thus glorying I fain would see
Mine enemies: among whom I number thee

HERMES.

What blame should I bear for thine evil fate?


PROMETHEUS.

My thought is simple. All the gods I hate
Who, being themselves in bliss, thus torture me.


HERMES.

I had heard 'twas no light madness vexing thee!


PROMETHEUS.

To hate the hater is mad? Then mad am I


HERMES.

So proud in chains, what wert thou throned on high?


PROMETHEUS (*bowing his head*).

Woe's me!

HERMES.

That is a word Zeus knoweth not.


PROMETHEUS

By Time and Age full many things are taught.
                    [*He raises his head again.*


HERMES.

Small wisdom have they taught to thee withal.

PROMETHEUS.

True, or I ne'er had parleyed with a thrall.


HERMES.

Thou wilt not speak the word Zeus asks of thee?


PROMETHEUS.

Nay, more than words he hath deserved from me!


HERMES.

Mocking thou answerest me: am I a child?


PROMETHEUS.

Yea, verily: and a thing more dream-beguiled
Than any babe, who think'st to learn from me
My secret. By no craft, no subtlety
Of torment, shall Zeus make me speak before
This bondage of my shame be broke. Therefore,
Delay not; let his jaggèd flame be hurled,
With white-winged snow and earthquake let the world
Be racked till chaos come: I warn thee well,
Naught of all these shall move my lips to tell
What hour, what hand, shall cast him to the abyss.


HERMES.

Think! Is there profit in such speech as this?


PROMETHEUS.

I have thought; I resolved this, long ago.

68

#### HERMES.

O madman! Try, try even now to know
Thine own helpless misfortune, and be wise!

#### PROMETHEUS.

In vain thou troublest me, like one that cries
Against the sea-wave. Let no hope, no thought,
Come near to thee, that I for fear of aught
That Zeus deviseth, will turn woman-souled,
Or sue to him I have hated from of old
With hands prayer-grovelling like a girl in fear,
To grant me his mercy.—My resolve is clear.

#### HERMES.

Meseemeth I speak on, and speak in vain.
Thou softenest not, thou turnest not again
For all my pleading. Like an untamed horse
Thou wilt bite the curb and rage, and fight perforce
To break thy reins. Yet 'tis a comfortless
Hope that uplifts thee; and mere stubbornness
Of heart against the truth is a weak shield,
Weaker than nothing! . . . Hearken now, if yield
Thou wilt not, what a storm, what wave threefold
Of unescapèd ravin shall be rolled
Upon thee. First, this gulf of jaggèd rock
The Sire shall rend in twain with thunder-shock
And fire of lightning. Deep shalt thou be thrown
Below the earth, gripped by an arm of stone;
Till, when an age-long space of years is past,
Back to the light above thou rise at last,

And then—God help thee!—the Sire's wingèd hound,
The blood-red eagle ravening, wound by wound,
Shall tear thy giant corse, and shred by shred;
Day after day, unbidden, to be fed
He comes, and heavy-pinioned shall depart
Blood-gorgèd from thy gnawed and blackened heart.
Nor ever respite from these agonies
Shall come till One Immortal shall arise
To take on him thy pains, and down descend
To Hades and the darkness without end
Of Tartarus and death. . . . Oh, think again!
The word I bring thee is no menace vain,
But true to the uttermost. The Father's thought
Knows not the path of falsehood, nor shall aught
He speaketh fail to be fulfilled. Do thou
But raise thine eyes to see, and even now
Take thought within; nor ever dream to find
More help in the angry heart than the wise mind.


### LEADER.

O friend, we hold the words of Hermes good.
Yield as he begs thee; cast away that mood
Of stubbornness, and make the truth thy prize!
Ill counsel is dishonour to the wise.


### PROMETHEUS.

This tale he utters I have known
    Long since. 'Tis no unlooked-for fate
    If I be wronged by those I hate.

I care not. Let the fire be thrown,
Two-bladed, curling. Let the sound
  Of thunder and the agony
  Of warring tempests rack the sky,
Till hills, uprooted from the ground,
By his wild wind be tossed and riven.
  Let Zeus confound in mingled roar
  The paths of waves upon the shore
And orbits of the stars in heaven.
Be mine own body lifted high,
  As Fate's hard eddies turn, and hurled
  To the black void beneath the world!
Whate'er befalls, I shall not die.

#### HERMES.

These be the words, and this the thought—
  Ye hear him!—of a stricken brain.
  What lacketh it of madness plain,
This vaunting, and this rage distraught?

               [*Turning to the* CHORUS:

Away, ye Comforters! And bless
  Your flying feet! Away, before
  Your minds be palsied by the roar
Of God's red thunder merciless!

#### LEADER.

Find thou another voice, and more
  Beguiling, if thou seek'st to turn
Me and my sisters! All thy lore
  Is craven, and thy care we spurn

71

With him whatever must be borne
   I too will bear. Was I not taught
   To loathe a traitor? There is naught
    I hold in deeper scorn.


HERMES.

Remember what my words have been
   When ruin hath ye! Cast no blame
   On Fortune, nor of Zeus proclaim
He wrought you evil unforeseen.
Ye have chosen, and your choice ye know.—
   Through no surprise, no plotted ill,
   Entangled by your own blind will
To Atê's yawning net ye go!
   *[He rises on his winged feet and sails away: the*
      DAUGHTERS OF OCEAN *gather closer to*
      PROMETHEUS. *A wild storm begins.*


PROMETHEUS.

Lo, 'tis the deed, no more the word!—
   The earth is shaken. A deep crash
   Of thunder moans afar; there flash
White forks of lightning; dust upstirred
In whirling columns eddyeth by,
   While all the armies of the wind
   Strive each 'gainst each in passion blind,
And chaos is on sea and sky.
         *[The storm increases.*

72

Nearer it cometh; against me:
The blast of Zeus in terror strong!
'Tis here.—O Earth, O Mother mine
Most holy, O thou Sky divine,
Whose light is shed on all, ye see
This anguish and this wrong!

[*A fiery thunderbolt strikes the Rock, which descends to the abyss, bearing with it* PROMETHEUS *and the* DAUGHTERS OF OCEAN.

# NOTES

THE Scene can only be conjectured from the text. There is evidently a high rock in the background, which at the end of the play sinks, with Prometheus on it, into the abyss. Prometheus, it would seem, must be represented by a gigantic wooden figure, since Hephaistos has to "climb down" to get from his breast to his ankles, l. 74. The characters Kratos and Bia (Might and Force) come from Hesiod, *Theogony*, 385, where they "are never away from Zeus, neither in his sitting nor his going." They afterwards became regular attributes of sovereignty, like "the kingdom, the power and the glory." (*Five Stages of Greek Religion*, p. 191, note.)

P. 20, l. 13, My kinsman: Prometheus was a fire god, like Hephaistos, and shared the same altar. Hephaistos seems to feel no resentment at the theft of fire.

P. 20, l. 27, Hephaistos means that no one can ever save Prometheus; but his words are true in the sense that his redeemer, Heracles, was not yet born.

P. 20, l. 35, Hard in the early days: Afterwards Zeus "learns by suffering."

P. 25, l. 87, Prometheus does not speak till he is left alone. This soliloquy is broken up into four parts: iambic, anapaestic, iambic again, and mixed lyric. Probably there were pauses between, and the effect was to suggest a long passage of time.

# PROMETHEUS BOUND

P. 26, l. 115, Fragrance: a regular sign of a divine presence. Cf. *Hippolytus*, 1391.

P. 26, l. 128, Entry of the Chorus. The stage arrangements are curious. The Chorus, Ocean, and presumably the winged Hermes, all enter flying through the air; only Io enters on foot and on the level ground. ("Along the sand, beside the starving sea.") Also, while for a great part of the play the Chorus are stationary in their chariots, Io dances both at her entrance and exit. This is just the contrary of the usual practice.

P. 27, l. 137, Têthys, the wife of Ocean, who was the father of all rivers and fountains.

P. 28, l. 164, Brood of Ouranos: i.e. Cronos and the Titans, whom Zeus had cast out.

P. 28, l. 170, The doom I know: i.e. that Thetis, whom Zeus loves, will bear a son greater than his father. See below, p. 56.

P. 30, l. 211, Themis and Gaia: the goddess presiding over oracles was either Themis ("Ancient Custom" or "Right"), since normally an oracle when consulted told you what was "the right thing" to do in such and such an emergency, or else she was Gaia ("Earth"), because oracles usually came from chasms in the earth or from the heroes in their graves. Here the two are identified. (Distinguish Thĕmis, Right, from Thĕtis, the sea goddess, and from Têthys, the wife of Ocean.)

P. 30, l. 218, I with Zeus: the Forethinker naturally was on the side of Zeus, the wise, as against the mere strength of the Titans.

# NOTES

P. 32, l. 253, Hath man fire?: to the Chorus also fire seems a divine thing.

P. 34, Enter Ocean: He exchanges no word with his daughters. This suggests that the crane which brought on his griffin at the same time swept off the Chorus on their chariots. The instrument had perhaps two arms, balancing one another. It seems that, when "off," the Chorus alight on some high place among the rocks and come forward on their feet.

Pp. 34–39, ll. 286–398, The object of this scene is not so much to let us see how Prometheus's friends fail him, as to show how Prometheus rejects all intercessions on his behalf and is determined not to involve others in his own suffering. Ocean comes eager to help, and confident that Zeus, whose ally he had been in the Titan war, will be gracious to him. He is shaken by the reminder that he has shared Prometheus's plans, and by the fates of Atlas and Typhon, but persists in his intention of pleading with Zeus until he is made to realize that Zeus will think that Prometheus has sent him. After that it would be a betrayal of Prometheus if he went. Still, we cannot but contrast his behaviour with that of his daughters.

P. 37, ll. 348–354, Atlas was a Titan. The hundred-headed monster, Typhon, or Typhôeus, was an ally of the Titans against Zeus. Where people found a volcano—at Arimi in Cilicia or at Etna in Sicily—it was Typhon imprisoned below and breathing fire. The prophecy must refer to the great eruption of 479 B.C.

77

P. 40, ll. 397 ff., This expression of the sympathy of all nature with the sufferings of the Saviour or Champion is very remarkable. It recurs in certain Christian conceptions—for example in the ideas of certain ascetic orders who try to share the passion of Christ—and in the Stoic doctrine of the συμπαθεία τῶν ὅλων, according to which the whole universe suffers with the suffering, or the sin, of any part of it. The next Chorus contains ideas somewhat akin.

P. 41, l. 436, I am silent: apparently there was some delay in the action here. Possibly it took the Chorus some time to return to their position.

Pp. 41–43, ll. 436–506, The story of Prometheus's services to mankind is interesting from many points of view. In the first speech we have the externals of civilization; in the second, services which seemed more intellectual: medicine, prophecy of various kinds, by dreams, by augury, by entrails, by fire, and lastly the art of mining. Observe how seriously Aeschylus here treats the art of prophecy; elsewhere in tragedy there is a good deal of scepticism about it.

P 45, l. 526, Chorus. A wonderful lyric. "I wish that I could always live in peace and piety, obeying the laws and adoring the gods: but suddenly I see the oppressions of the world and my conscience rebels. Yet how can Man, in his weakness, rise against Zeus, i.e. against the whole non-human world order?"—The bride of Prometheus was Hesione, daughter of Ocean.

P. 46, l. 561, Io. On Io, the horned Moon-maiden, loved by Zeus, persecuted by Hera, driven across the sky and watched by the innumerable eyes of the stars, see the *Suppliant Women*, Introduction. She was the daughter of the River Inachus, who, like all rivers, was a son of Ocean. The Watcher, Argos, had been slain by Hermes, but his ghost still watches her. She cries to Zeus ("O Thou Eternal"), her lover and persecutor, for mercy.

P. 53, l. 717, River named of wrath: the Araxes.

Pp. 53–61, ll. 700–876, Io is a moving and imaginative figure, but the three speeches of Prometheus about her wanderings strike us as undramatic. The age of Aeschylus was enormously interested in voyages of discovery and accounts of strange lands. (Cf. *Suppliant Women*, ll. 250 ff.) We have, first, Io's future wandering till she leaves Europe (735); then her more mythical wanderings through Asia and down the Nile (814); then the beginning of her past journeys by Dodona and the Ionian Gulf and the prophecy of what shall happen after she has reached her home at Canôpus— the healing hand of Zeus, the birth of Epaphos, the story of the Daughters of Danaus, who slew their ravishers, and the ultimate release of Prometheus by Heracles. This part of the story, touched lightly here, is treated in the *Suppliant Women* as the key to the mystery. In it the purpose of Zeus is revealed.

P. 61, l. 864, One alone: Hypermnestra spared Lynceus because she loved him, and thereby broke the oath which all the Danaids had sworn. She it is whom Horace calls "splendide mendax."

P. 62, ll. 887 ff., Stories of the loves of gods for the

daughters of men are, of course, common in Greek legend. In this interesting lyric we have an effort to realize what such stories mean, and the shrinking of the mortal woman from an intolerable exaltation. Compare, in different ways, Semelê, who died from the fiery splendour of the presence of Zeus, and Marpessa, loved by Apollo, who could not forget her human lover.

P. 64, l. 936, Literally, "wise are they who prostrate themselves before Adrasteia." Adrasteia ("Inescapable") was another name for Nemesis.

P. 66, l. 970, Scorn for scorn: if the text is sound this must mean that only when nailed to the rock, having nothing worse to fear, can Prometheus fully show his scorn for the life that he has rejected.

P. 70, l. 1027, Till one immortal shall arise: a reference to the version of the legend in which Chiron, the divine Centaur, suffering from the incurable wound of an arrow of Heracles, agreed to die in place of Prometheus. It does not seem that Aeschylus actually used that version: perhaps the reconciliation with Zeus made such sacrifice unnecessary.

Pp. 70–73, ll. 1036–1063, A very fine end. Those who love the Suffering Deliverer are cast into torment with him, and the last words of the play are a testification to the injustice of the world. Zeus may say, "I cast you to Hell if you call me unjust," but that is no proof of his justice.